3 9082 10130 4817

D1218960

THE WORLD'S GREATEST
TRUCKS AND EARTHMOVERS

Ian Graham

Raintree

Chicago, Illinois

For more information address the publisher:
Raintree, 100 N. LaSalle, Suite 1200, Chicago,
IL 60602

Editorial: Andrew Farrow and Dan Nunn
Design: Ron Kamen and Philippa Baile
Picture Research: Hannah Taylor and Elaine
  Willis
Production: Duncan Gilbert

Originated by Dot Gradations Ltd.
Printed in China

The paper used to print this book comes from
sustainable resources.

10 09 08 07 06
10 9 8 7 6 5 4 3 2 1

**Library of Congress Cataloging-in-
Publication Data**
Graham, Ian, 1953-
  Trucks and earthmovers / Ian Graham.
    p. cm. -- (The World's greatest)
  Includes bibliographical references and
index.
  ISBN 1-4109-2088-7 (library binding-
hardcover) -- ISBN 1-4109-2095-X (pbk.)
  1. Earthmoving machinery--Juvenile
literature. [1. Trucks--Juvenile literature.]
I. Title. II. Series.

TA725.G69 2005
629.224--dc22
                                2005016370

Acknowledgments
The publishers would like to thank the
following for permission to reproduce
photographs:

Bert Visser Dredgers p. **25**; Corbis pp. **4** (Craig
Aurness), **5 top** (Lester Lefkowitz), **5 bottom**
(Sandro Vannini), **8** (Reuters/Tim Wimborne),
9 (Bennett Dean/Eye Ubiquitous), **10** (Ed
Kashi); Komatsu pp. **16**, **17 top**, **17 bottom**,
22; LeTourneau Inc pp. **14**, **15**; Leibherr France
SAS pp. **1**, **12**, **13**, **24**; Man Takraf pp. **18**, **19**;
O&K pp. **20**, **21**; Oshkosh p. **11**; P&H Mining
Equipment p. **23**; Peterbilt p. **6**; Volvo pp. **7
top**, **7 bottom**.

Cover photograph reproduced with permission
of ATM Images.

Every effort has been made to contact
copyright holders of any material reproduced
in this book. Any omissions will be rectified in
subsequent printings if notice is given to the
publishers.

Contents

Some words are shown in bold, **like this**. You can find out
what they mean by looking in the glossary.

Trucks and Earthmovers

Trucks are vehicles that carry all the things we eat, wear, and use. Trucks transport raw materials to factories to make things like clothes and toys. Trucks also carry these things from the factories to shops. They transport food from farms to factories and shops, too.

Off-road giants

Most of the trucks we see are on roads. But huge trucks and digging machines also work at mines and construction sites. They move large amounts of dirt, coal, and rock. Some trucks have to share the roads with other vehicles. Big diggers and earthmovers do not travel on highways. They can be much bigger than road trucks. Some of them are giant vehicles.

Trucks transport goods and materials all over the country.

Trucks and earthmovers move huge amounts of coal, dirt, and rock out of mines.

Trucks carry produce from farms to markets. They also move goods to cities and towns.

The Greatest Road Trucks

Trucks have to carry heavy loads for long distances. They need powerful engines. The biggest trucks on our roads are called big rigs in the United States, artics in the United Kingdom, and semis in Australia.

These big trucks have two parts. The front part with the engine is called the tractor. The tractor is then connected to a semi-trailer. This lets the truck bend in the middle. It also lets a tractor unhook a load and pick up another load quickly and easily.

The Peterbilt Model 379 is a long-nosed big rig. It is used throughout the United States and Canada.

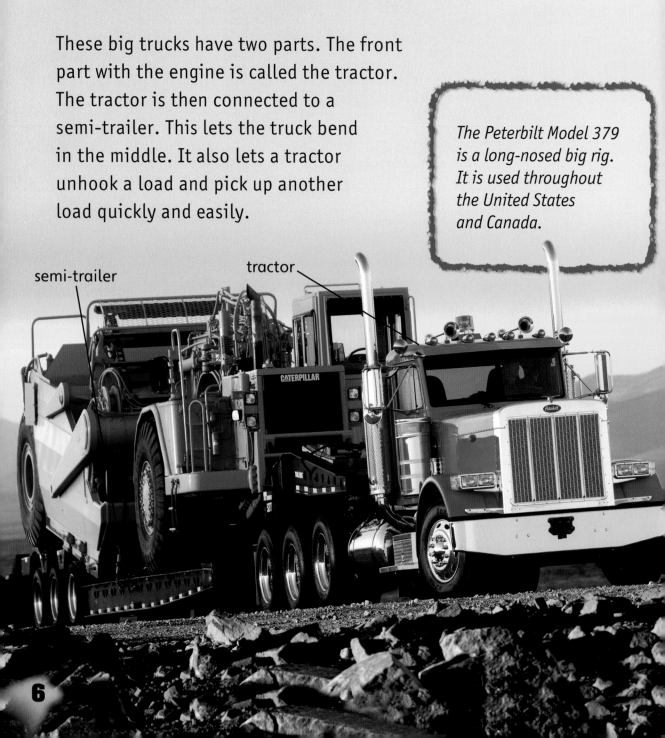

semi-trailer

tractor

Trucks with flat fronts are more common in Europe than in the United States. They are called cabovers. The driver sits above the engine.

Types of trucks

Some trucks are made to carry one type of cargo. For example, tanker trucks carry liquids such as milk, oil, and gasoline. Refrigerated trucks keep fresh food cold. Car transporters carry cars on a special double-deck trailer.

The whole cab of a cabover truck can tilt forward if the engine needs to be repaired.

engine

 Peterbilt Model 379 Big Rig Truck

BMW 316i Family Car

Engine:	891 cu. in./14.6 liters	110 cu. in./1.8 liters
Power:	up to 625 horsepower	115 horsepower
Weight:	40 tons fully loaded	1.4 tons

A big rig with a full load weighs as much as 28 cars.

The Longest Road Trucks

The longest trucks in the world drive up and down Australia's dusty roads. They are called road trains. Most Australians live in a few cities around the coast. Goods have to be moved great distances between these cities. This is done by road trains.

Prime movers

Most road trains have a tractor, called the prime mover. This pulls three or four trailers. Some road trains are even longer. Each trailer is as long as three cars. This is a very heavy load to pull, so prime movers of road trains are far more powerful than most truck tractors.

LONG VEHICLE
A road train with three trailers is as long as 11 cars.

Road trains like this one move goods all over Australia.

Don't run out of fuel!

There are very few **fuel** stations on the long roads in Australia. Road trains carry enough fuel for about 1,000 miles (1,600 kilometers). They often travel in groups called convoys. This is so a road train that breaks down always has help nearby.

Australian Road Train

Length:	**174 ft./53 m**
Trailers:	**3**
Load Pulled:	**154.3 tons**
Engine:	**650 horsepower**
Speed:	**60 mph/100 kph**

Road trains have strong bars across the front. The bars protect them from damage if they hit a wild animal. The bars are called bull bars, but drivers are more likely to find kangaroos than bulls on the road!

The Biggest Army Movers

Armies have to move lots of heavy equipment, such
as tanks. They need big, powerful trucks. The
biggest trucks used by the army are the Oshkosh
HETs. HET stands for Heavy Equipment Transporter.

The super-trailer

The HET is a powerful tractor unit. It pulls special
military trailers. The trailers have ramps at the back
that can be lowered for loading vehicles. Up to 40
wheels share their heavy weight over the road.
Some of the wheels turn to steer the trailer when
the driver turns the tractor's steering wheel.

The HET's main job is to take
tanks and other military
vehicles to wherever the
army needs them.

Tank transporter

The Oshkosh HET carries tanks such as the United States Abrams tank. Each of these large battle tanks weighs as much as 50 cars! The HET can carry other heavy loads too, such as **artillery** guns and armored cars. It can travel by road or across rough ground. The front and back wheels steer to help it get round tight turns.

The HET has to go wherever the army needs it. Sometimes there are no roads to get there.

Oshkosh 1070F HET

Engine:	**700 horsepower diesel**
Weight:	**49.5 tons**
Fully Loaded Weight:	**130.1 tons**
Speed (carrying a tank):	**30 mph/48 kph**

The Biggest Dump Truck

The biggest trucks do not drive on public roads, like streets and highways. They carry away the soil and rock from mines and construction sites. These huge trucks are called **dump trucks**. The biggest dump truck is the Liebherr T-282B.

Ultra trucks

The T-282B is so high that the driver needs a ladder to reach the cab. It is so wide and long that the driver has to use video cameras to see around it! The T-282B can carry nearly 25 times more earth than a small dump truck that goes on a public road. Trucks like the T-282B are so big that they are also called Ultra Trucks. The word *ultra* means beyond or extreme.

A Liebherr T-282B with a full load is so heavy that the ground shakes as it rumbles past.

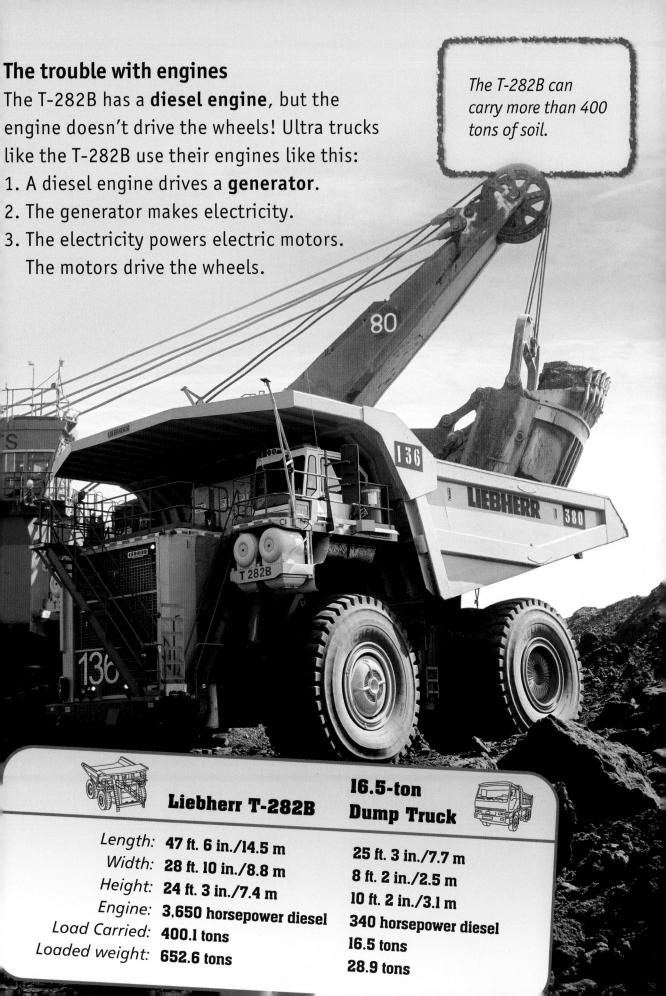

The trouble with engines

The T-282B has a **diesel engine**, but the engine doesn't drive the wheels! Ultra trucks like the T-282B use their engines like this:

1. A diesel engine drives a **generator**.
2. The generator makes electricity.
3. The electricity powers electric motors. The motors drive the wheels.

The T-282B can carry more than 400 tons of soil.

	Liebherr T-282B	16.5-ton Dump Truck
Length:	47 ft. 6 in./14.5 m	25 ft. 3 in./7.7 m
Width:	28 ft. 10 in./8.8 m	8 ft. 2 in./2.5 m
Height:	24 ft. 3 in./7.4 m	10 ft. 2 in./3.1 m
Engine:	3,650 horsepower diesel	340 horsepower diesel
Load Carried:	400.1 tons	16.5 tons
Loaded weight:	652.6 tons	28.9 tons

The Largest Loaders

Sometimes piles of dirt and rock on top of the ground have to be cleared away. Earthmovers called loaders do this job. The biggest loader is the LeTourneau L-2350. It can lift a bucket full of dirt that weighs more than 50 cars! It can lift the load as high as four people standing on each other's shoulders.

LeTourneau L-2350 Loader

Engine:	2,300 horsepower diesel
Weight:	289 tons
Bucket-load:	79.5 tons

*Giant loaders like the L-2350 have enormous tires. The deep **grooves** in the tires help them to grip the ground.*

An L-2350 loader could easily lift a 75-ton army tank.

Scooping dirt

The L-2350 has to scoop up a lot of dirt. It has a wide bucket at the front. The vehicle drives toward the pile of earth and pushes the bucket into it. The bucket is lifted up. It is also tilted back so that nothing falls out. It has to be lifted high enough to go over the top of a dump truck. Then the bucket is tilted down and the dirt falls into the truck.

The biggest loaders are designed to load the biggest trucks as fast as possible.

The Biggest Bulldozer

Bulldozers move dirt by pushing it. This is called dozing. The bulldozer has a blade at the front. This pushes the dirt along.

Super-Dozer

The biggest bulldozer is the Komatsu D575A. This is so big and powerful that it is sometimes called a Super-Dozer. It can move more dirt at one time than any other bulldozer. It is more than twice as big and heavy as the world's biggest army tanks.

blade

Komatsu D575A
Super-Dozer

Engine:	1,050 horsepower diesel
Weight:	168.2 tons
Blade Width:	24 ft. 3 in./7.4 m
Blade Height:	10 ft. 6 in./3.2 m

The Super-Dozer's blade can be lowered or raised. It is lowered to scrape up more dirt. It is raised to push less dirt.

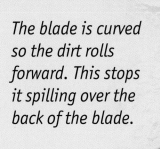

The blade is curved so the dirt rolls forward. This stops it spilling over the back of the blade.

Staying on track

Bulldozers run on **tracks** instead of wheels. Tracks spread their weight over more ground. This stops them sinking into soft dirt. Tracks also grip the ground well. This means that bulldozers can push heavy piles of dirt.

BIG BLADE

The blade on the front of the Komatsu D575A is as long as two cars. It is more than twice as high, too.

ripper

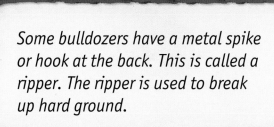

Some bulldozers have a metal spike or hook at the back. This is called a ripper. The ripper is used to break up hard ground.

The Greatest Land Vehicle

The greatest vehicle that travels on land is a giant earthmover. It makes all other trucks and earthmovers look tiny.

A giant among giants

The MAN TAKRAF RB293 is a bucket wheel **excavator** that digs coal out of the ground in Germany. It is the biggest earthmover. It is also the biggest land machine that can move under its own power. It is as tall as the Statue of Liberty in New York. It also weighs more than 10,000 cars.

The bucket wheel hangs from the end of an arm. This is called a boom. When the boom is lowered, the buckets cut into the ground.

boom

bucket wheel

Scooping up coal

The giant excavator works by pushing a huge wheel into the ground. The wheel has buckets around it. As the wheel turns, the buckets cut into the ground and scoop up the coal. Each bucket is as big as a car!

As the wheel turns further, the coal spills out and lands on a **conveyor belt**. The moving belt carries it away. The RB293 can dig 40,000 buckets of coal in a day.

MAN TAKRAF RB293

Type:	Bucket wheel excavator
Length:	722 ft./220 m
Height:	310 ft./94.5 m
Wheel Diameter:	71 ft./21.6 m
Weight:	15,648.4 tons

The RB293 excavator moves on eight crawlers. It cuts a huge trench through the ground.

The Largest Hydraulic Excavator

Another huge earthmover is the Terex O & K RH400. It has a bucket on a long arm. It uses this to dig and scoop up earth. An experienced operator can move its bucket fast. It takes only about one minute to fill a giant dump truck with three bucket-loads of dirt. Each bucket-load of dirt scooped up by the RH400 weighs as much as 63 cars.

The RH400 is the largest **hydraulic** excavator in the world. It has tubes called hydraulic rams. Pumping oil into a ram pushes a rod out of one end. This moves the digger's mechanical arm.

Giant crawler

The RH400 moves on crawler tracks, like a tank. It travels only short distances around a mine. When an RH400 had to be moved to another mine in the state of Wyoming, it had to be carried there. Eight trailers were joined together to make a platform big enough for the excavator. The trailers had a total of 260 wheels. The excavator was moved so slowly and carefully that the 27-mile (43-kilometer) journey took three weeks!

Terex O & K RH400

Type:	Hydraulic excavator
Weight:	1080.3 tons
Engine Power:	4,400 horsepower
Bucket-load:	93.7 tons

The RH400 is operated by two small hand controls that are like video game joysticks.

Other Big Diggers

One of the world's biggest diggers is the giant Komatsu PC8000. The Komatsu PC8000 is built for mining. Its bucket can scoop up enough dirt to fill 117 bathtubs! It can move around at walking pace on two huge crawler tracks. PC8000s are used in mines all over the world.

> The PC8000 is so big that the driver sits as high as the third floor of a building.

	Komatsu PC8000	P & H 4100XPB
Type:	Hydraulic excavator	Cable-operated excavator
Power:	4,020 horsepower	7,900 horsepower
Weight:	799.9 tons	1,543.2 tons
Bucket-load:	75 tons	114.6 tons

Speedy digger

The PC8000 is tiny compared to the much bigger P & H 4100XPB. It digs coal in a mine in Wyoming.
The 4100XPB is called a cable-operated excavator because its bucket hangs on the end of cables. The machine can move its bucket fast. It can scoop up dirt and rock weighing more than 75 cars and drop them into a truck in less than 29 seconds.

The 4100XPB is so big that it has to be transported in pieces. It takes three months to put all the pieces together.

Big Backhoes

A digging machine can use its bucket to dig in two different ways. It can push the bucket away from it, like a shovel. Or, it can pull the bucket back toward it, scooping up earth on the way. A bucket that is pulled toward a digger is called a **backhoe**.

The Liebherr 996 can be fitted with a shovel or a backhoe. In this photo, it is fitted with a backhoe.

Digging trenches

Backhoes are good for digging trenches. They can dig down deeper than shovels. Some giant diggers can be fitted with a backhoe instead of a shovel. The Liebherr 996 is one of the biggest.

Floating diggers

Most backhoes are used on dry land, but some float on barges. They clear gravel and mud from the bottom of harbors and water channels. This allows ships to sail through safely. Digging under water like this is called dredging.

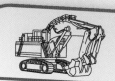

Liebherr R996 Litronic	
Type:	**Hydraulic excavator**
Power:	**3,000 horsepower**
Weight:	**736.3 tons**
Backhoe	
Bucket-load:	**64.8 tons**
Shovel load:	**66.8 tons**

This Liebherr 996 floats on a barge in New York Harbor. Its backhoe digs nearly 56 feet (17 meters) below the water to deepen the harbor for ships.

Facts and Figures

There are hundreds of trucks and earthmovers. Some of the biggest and most powerful are listed here. You can use the information to see which can move the most dirt or carry the heaviest loads.

If you want to find out more about these or other trucks and earthmovers, read the section called Further Information on pages 30 and 31.

Road Truck Tractors

Name	Engine	Horsepower	Tractor Weight	Truck Weight (loaded)
Mack CX600 Vision	732 cu. in./12 liters	460 horsepower	16.5 tons	40 tons
Peterbilt Model 379	891 cu. in./14.6 liters	up to 625 h.p.	16.4 tons	40 tons
Scania T144L	867 cu. in./14.2 liters	530 horsepower	20.9 tons	40 tons
Western Star 4964SX	891 cu. in./14.6 liters	355 horsepower	16.4 tons	40 tons

Dump Trucks

Name	Power	Payload	Loaded Weight
Caterpillar 797	3,224 horsepower	359.4 tons	614.9 tons
Liebherr T-282B	3,650 horsepower	400.1 tons	652.6 tons

Special Trucks

Name	Vehicle Type	Power	Loaded Weight
Oshkosh 1070F HET	Military transporter	700 horsepower	130.1 tons
Western Star Constellation 4964EX	Australian road train	650 horsepower	154.3 tons

Diggers and Earthmovers

Name	Vehicle Type	Weight	Power	Bucket-load
Big Muskie	Dragline excavator	13,227.7 tons	62,600 horsepower	330.7 tons
Komatsu D575A	Bulldozer	168.2 tons	1,050 horsepower	106.2 tons *
Komatsu PC8000	Hydraulic excavator	800 tons	4,020 horsepower	75 tons
LeTourneau L-2350	Front-end loader	289 tons	2,300 horsepower	79.5 tons
Liebherr R996	Hydraulic excavator	736.3 tons	3,000 horsepower	66.8 tons
MAN TAKRAF RB293	Bucket wheel excavator	15,648.4 tons	Unknown	Unknown
P & H 4100XPB	Cable-operated excavator	1,543.2 tons	7,900 horsepower	114.6 tons
Terex O & K RH400	Hydraulic excavator	1,080.3 tons	4,400 horsepower	93.7 tons
The Captain	Power shovel	13,999.4 tons	21,000 horsepower	270.1 tons

* The amount of dirt the bulldozer's blade can push.

Big Muskie

The biggest single-bucket digging machine ever built was called Big Muskie. It was a **dragline excavator**. Big Muskie started work in 1969 in the United States. It was as tall as a 22-story building. It weighed 13,228 tons—that's as much as thirty 747-400 Jumbo Jet airliners! Its bucket was big enough to park 12 cars inside. Big Muskie did not have wheels or crawler tracks. Instead, it walked on huge feet. Big Muskie was shut down for the last time in 1991.

The Captain

The biggest stripping shovel ever made was called the Captain. A stripping shovel is a digger used in a strip mine. A strip mine is a mine where the coal or other valuable material is just below the surface. The Captain was so big that trucks could drive underneath it while it was working. It weighed nearly 14,000 tons. It dug coal in the state of Illinois starting in 1965. It was destroyed by fire in 1991.

Glossary

artillery large military weapon that fires exploding shells. It is also called a field gun.

backhoe bucket on a digging machine that is lowered onto the ground and pulled back toward the machine

conveyer belt an moving loop or band, used to move material from place to place

cu. in. cubic inch. A space that is one inch long, high, and wide. The space inside an engine where the fuel is burned is sometimes measured in cubic inches (cu in).

diesel engine engine that burns diesel oil. Most trucks and earthmoving machines have diesel engines.

dragline excavator type of digging machine. It lowers a bucket onto the ground and uses cables to pull it along and fill it up.

dump truck truck that tips up. The earth or rock piled up inside it slides out through the tailgate. Dump trucks are also called tipper trucks.

excavator another name for a digging machine

fuel substance that is burned in an engine to power a truck. Most trucks have diesel engines. They burn a fuel called diesel oil.

generator a machine that makes electricity

groove channel cut into something. Deep grooves in truck tires help them to grip soft ground.

horsepower the power of an engine

hydraulic worked by liquid. Hydraulic digging machines move their mechanical arms by pumping oil into tubes called rams. This makes the rams extend, causing the mechanical arms to move.

tailgate back end of a truck. Some dump trucks and tipper trucks have a tailgate that can be unlocked. When the back of the truck tips up, the tailgate swings open. The load then slides out onto the ground.

tracks metal belts, like flattened bicycle chains, that go round a bulldozer's wheels. Tracks spread a bulldozer's weight more evenly over the ground and help it grip the earth.

Further Information

You can find out more information about trucks and earthmovers by reading the following books about these subjects.

Books to read

Bingham, Caroline. *Big Book of Trucks*. New York: Dorling Kindersley Children, 1999.

Bruun, Erik. *Kids' Book of Giant Machines*. New York: Black Dog & Leventhal Publishers, 2000.

Deschamps, Nicola. *Digger: Machines at Work*. New York: Dorling Kindersley Children, 2004.

Graham, Ian. *Designed for Success: Off-Road Vehicles*. Chicago: Heinemann Library, 2004.

Nelson, Kristin L. *Monster Trucks*. Minneapolis: Lerner Publishing Group, 2002.

Places to visit

Caterpillar Production Facility

Visit Clayton or Sanford, North Carolina to see how earthmovers are made! You can visit the Backhoe Loader Advantage Showroom to see how Caterpillar's machines compare to other machines on the market.

Mack Museum

Visit Allentown, Pennsylvania to view the "Wheels of Time" exhibit of Mack trucks from 1907 to 1973. If you'd like to see how heavy-duty trucks are made, you've come to the right place! You can also visit the Macungie Assembly Operations in Macungie, Pennsylvania to see how the larger trucks are manufactured.

Index